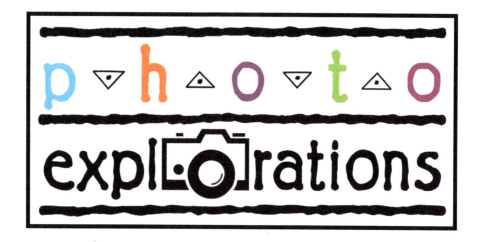

A Girl's Guide to Self-Discovery Through Photography, Writing and Drawing

CATHY LANDER-GOLDBERG, MSW, LCSW

PHOTO EXPLORATIONS:
A Girl's Guide to Self-Discovery Through Photography, Writing and Drawing

Cathy Lander-Goldberg, MSW, LCSW

Publisher Name: CLG Photographics, Inc.

Published by: *CLG Photographics, Inc.*
St. Louis, Missouri USA

Copyright ©2015 Cathy Lander-Goldberg
All rights reserved.

No part of this publication may be reproduced, stored in a retrieval system, or transmitted in any form or by any means, electronic, mechanical, photocopying, recording, scanning, or otherwise, except as permitted under Section 107 or 108 of the 1976 United States Copyright Act, without the prior written permission of the Publisher. Requests to the Publisher for permission should be sent to photoexplorationsCLG@gmail.com.

Limit of Liability/Disclaimer of Warranty: While the publisher and author have used their best efforts in preparing this book, they make no representations or warranties with respect to the accuracy or completeness of the contents of this book and specifically disclaim any implied warranties of merchantability or fitness for a particular purpose. No warranty may be created or extended by sales representatives or written sales materials.

The advice and strategies contained herein may not be suitable for your situation. You should consult with a professional where appropriate. Neither the publisher nor author shall be liable for any loss of profit or any other commercial damages, including but not limited to special, incidental, consequential, or other damages.

Logo design by Richard Meehan
Book Production and Design Consultants: Davis Creative, www.DavisCreative.com

Library of Congress Cataloging-in-Publication Data
Library of Congress Control Number: 2015917557

Lander-Goldberg, Cathy
PHOTO EXPLORATIONS:
A Girl's Guide to Self-Discovery Through Photography, Writing and Drawing

ISBN: 978-0-692-52970-6

Library of Congress subject headings:
1. Juvenile Nonfiction/Girls & Women 2. Photography
   3. Social Issues/Self-Esteem & Self-Reliance

Publication year: 2015

For information, please contact:
PHOTO EXPLORATIONS, a division of CLG Photographics, Inc.
St. Louis, MO USA photoexplorationsCLG@gmail.com

This book is dedicated

to my amazing daughter, Danielle,

and all of the incredible girls

(of all ages) I have had the

honor of working with and knowing.

Table of Contents:

Introduction: 5

Chapter 1 - A Look Back at Me 12
- Use old photos to remember and make discoveries about your past.
- Re-visit your experiences and write about growing up.

Chapter 2 - My Family 16
- Create a collage about your family.
- Write about your family and your special connections within it.

Chapter 3 - My Home, Neighborhood and Community 20
- Create a photo essay about your home.
- Reflect upon the area where you live.

Chapter 4 - My Friends 24
- Take a look at your social circle.
- Explore any changes you may like to see happen.
- Consider how your friends may view you.

Chapter 5 - My Strengths and Accomplishments 28
- Examine your internal positive qualities.
- Highlight one of these qualities with an image.

Chapter 6 - My Worries & Challenges 31
- Make a collage about your current worries.
- Reflect on your self-talk about these worries.
- Take or draw a picture of yourself when relaxed and one when you are stressed.
- Review a past or current challenge

Chapter 7 - Balance in My Life 37
- Learn how your mind and body are connected.
- Consider actions you may take to care for your physical and emotional needs.
- Write a letter to your body.

Chapter 8 - Meaning in My Life 41
- Explore words and possessions that are significant to you.
- Reflect on your role models.
- Examine causes that you consider worthwhile.

Chapter 9 - The Real Me - Who is the True You? 47
- Consider different roles you play in your life and create a self-portrait to show the "real" you.
- Write about allowing others to see the true you.

Chapter 10 - The Future Me 50
- Design an image of the "future" you.
- Explore your goals.
- Plan tasks to help your goals become a reality.

Acknowledgements: 56
References 57
About the Author: 59

**"Always be a first-rate version of yourself,
instead of a second-rate version of somebody else."**
~Judy Garland (who played Dorothy in the *Wizard of Oz*)

Introduction:

Dear Readers,

Growing up is a time to discover who you are and who you want to become. The activities in this book will help you learn more about what makes you unique. You will be asked to find and take photos of yourself, others and your environment (or draw them) and answer questions about the pictures. This book uses images to explore your family and friends and the roles you play. It also will help you examine your past and current life as well as consider your future goals and encourage you to create a plan to achieve them. I hope you have as much fun working in your book as I had writing it!

PHOTO EXPLORATIONS

YOU WILL NEED:

Colorful pencils, pens or thin markers (Thick or permanent markers may show through to the next page.)
A glue stick or double stick tape
A pair of scissors
Old magazines if you want to clip out photos or words for your collages
A camera or cell phone that takes photos

The ability to print the photos you take. There are many on-line sites and stores that offer low prices and "deals" on printing photos. If you do not have a camera, you could draw your portraits or use <u>copies</u> (not originals) of photos you already have. Remember to ask permission from parents to copy or scan and print family photos. (For a fun look, you may want to make black and white copies of color photos and use markers to color parts of the image any way you like.)

6

TIPS FOR TAKING PHOTOS:

Take a moment to imagine how you want the final image to look and experiment by using different angles and backgrounds. That way, you will have a selection of images to choose from. You may want to consider a "bird's eye" view, which means taking the photo from above looking down or a "worm's eye" view, which means getting down on the ground and looking up at your subject. You may choose to shoot close up if your camera allows that option or from further away.

PHOTO EXPLORATIONS

EXPERIMENT WITH LIGHTING:

For indoor shots, try letting in more natural light from a window or adjusting room lights. (**Note:** taking photos in low light situations may lower the quality of your images.) Outdoor photos tend to be brighter and clearer with many cameras. Also, know that the quality of the light changes throughout the day, so see what you like best. Usually, right after sunrise or before sunset is beautiful.

PHOTO EXPLORATIONS

TIPS FOR SELF-PORTRAITS:

You could. . .

- ▶ photograph yourself in the mirror or other reflective surface (with the flash turned off to avoid glare).
- ▶ use a self-timer or "selfie" remote by placing the camera on a flat surface or tripod.

- ▶ ask a parent or friend to press the button and you plan out everything else about the photo so they are taking the photo you want.
- ▶ take a "selfie" with a cell phone or camera. (Remember, sometimes the angles are awkward and your arm cannot extend far enough away to include all of you so you may want to use a Selfie Stick to place your phone further away.)

In self-portraits, try not to focus on your hair being "just right" or smiling perfectly in all the images. (You probably have plenty of those pictures already.) Since in real life, you are not always smiling, use this opportunity to explore the many different ways your mood and personality appear.

9

PHOTO EXPLORATIONS

TIPS FOR WRITING ABOUT THE PICTURES:

▶ Try to respond honestly to the questions about the photos without trying to make your answers sound perfect or worrying about what others may think of your writing.

▶ If for some reason, you dislike something about your appearance in the photo, try to focus on what you do like about the photo rather than listening to a negative thought.

Perfectionism and CREATIVITY:

Sometimes when we are about to design or write something, a critical voice in our head tells us "that's stupid" or "that's not good enough". I encourage you to ignore that voice because it blocks your expression! We all like to do our best but the activities in this book are to help you learn more about yourself — not to judge yourself. Please give yourself permission to write your thoughts (without worrying what others will think) and to create without trying to make your art, collage, writing or photos PERFECT. If you make a mistake, use it as an opportunity to turn it into something even more imaginative! And, if you would like to use your unique ideas to change a suggested activity or do the assignments out of order, please do!

THIS IS YOUR BOOK!

PRIVACY:

In the following activities, you will be asked to write about your personal beliefs, which you may or may not choose to share with everyone. Think about who you will allow to see your book and consider a safe, private place to keep it. You may decide it would be helpful for you to work with a parent or another trustworthy person. Who you choose to share your work with is your decision but if an activity brings up strong feelings that you find highly uncomfortable, I encourage you to talk with an adult or school counselor who can help you understand them better. Thinking of the past or future may trigger a variety of feelings such as sadness, fear, worry, excitement, anger and confusion. Remember, all of these feelings are acceptable but when feelings are very upsetting to you, it is a good idea to discuss them with a trusted adult.

CHAPTER 1
A Look Back at Me

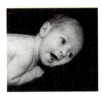

Create a collage on these pages using 5 or more (copies) of photos of important times in your childhood – for example, photos of you as a baby, the 1st day at a new school, or on special occasions.
(See back cover for example.)

PHOTO EXPLORATIONS

You may choose to include other people in this collage but we will "focus" more on family and friend pictures later in Chapters 2 and 4. (If you don't have access to old photos, you may find images online or in magazines that remind you of your younger years. Or, you may draw them.)

Look at your collage and think about your life up to this age you are now. Write about your favorite childhood memories here:

Write about anything you miss about your childhood:

Write about something you do not miss about your childhood:

As you look back on your experiences and what you have learned about the world, what advice would you give a younger girl about growing up?

CHAPTER 2
My Family

Attach one or more photos of whoever you consider your "family":

PHOTO EXPLORATIONS

Write about what your family thinks is important. How does your family spend time? Do you come from a family who is focused on playing sports or attending games on the weekend? Does your family enjoy watching funny movies together? Do all of you like to hike in nature, visit the library or cook a special meal together? Do you spend lots of free time with other relatives? Are you involved with your church, temple or mosque?

Write about a favorite family memory:

Describe what you appreciate about your family and hope will not change:

Is there something you hope to be different about your family in the future?

PHOTO EXPLORATIONS

For each family member with whom you feel a special connection to, write about the things you like to do together on this page. You may choose to add photos or drawings of you participating in that activity with your relative.

CHAPTER 3
My Home, Neighborhood and Community

MY ROOM

My Home: Create a collage of photos about your home. Use your vision to take pictures with a variety of angles and lighting. Also, try getting details that help tell the story. For example, you could take close-ups of your mailbox, the items on your refrigerator door or your toothbrushes in the bathroom you share with your siblings.

PHOTO EXPLORATIONS

MY HOME

You may try shooting pictures from inside showing your view and going outdoors to get the exterior of your apartment or house. Include things you want to remember about your home in years to come. If you live in two separate homes, show each one. Select the best images and make a collage on these two pages. (Or, draw pictures or a map of your home.)

PHOTO EXPLORATIONS

MY NEIGHBORHOOD & COMMUNITY

MY FAVORITE PARK!

This space is for photos or drawings of things in your community. Consider pictures of your school, a park, a landmark or a favorite sports team.

PHOTO EXPLORATIONS

Write about what you appreciate about your neighborhood and/or community:

What would you like to see changed in your neighborhood and/or community:

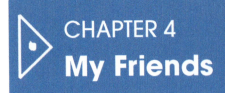

CHAPTER 4
My Friends

Create a friend collage. First, place a photo of you in the center of the page. Then, draw or cut out and glue pictures of your pals around you. You may choose to place the people you feel most connected to closer to your photo.

(**Note:** Remember, you may also want to include those who don't go to your school but you know from other areas of your life such as the neighborhood, sports or religious youth groups. Also, feel free to include friends of all ages—even the 4-legged kind.)

Next, review your collage and write your responses to these questions:

What qualities do the friends closest to you have that make you feel close or connected to them?

What, if anything, has changed about your friendships in the last year or two and how do you feel about this?

How do you think your friends see you? (This is your interpretation, so you do not need to ask your friends but guess how you think they view you.)

For the next assignment, take a self-portrait of how you think your closest friends see you. (See example below.) Place your photo on the next page:

"I think my friends see me as funny but also too silly sometimes."

PHOTO EXPLORATIONS

TITLE:

In the picture, I'm trying to show that my friends see me as:

If there is anything you would like to be different about how your friends see you, what might that be? (Using the example of "silly", would you prefer your friends also see that you can be serious at times?) If there is nothing you want to be different about how they see you, that's fine. Go ahead and move on to Chapter 5.

Think about how you could change this? What actions might you take to make this more likely to happen? (Using the example above, if you wanted your friends to see you can be serious, would you try to be more thoughtful or concerned when they are troubled?)

CHAPTER 5
My Strengths and Accomplishments

What are your **accomplishments**?
(This is a place to list big and small achievements such as learning to swim, knit or ride a bike; singing a solo in choir; staying home alone; getting an "A" or maybe working hard to earn a "C" in a subject that was very difficult.)

What **qualities** are you proud of concerning how you treat others? Are you a good listener, a first-rate hugger, a loyal friend?

What are your **talents**? Are you a good at babysitting, creating videos, drawing, playing the flute, solving a problem, making people laugh? Do you have a style for fashion or a flair for writing? List any talents below. (If you are having trouble thinking of your talents, ask a parent or friend for help.)

MAKING MUSIC!
"I love playing my violin, and I am good at it!"
I like that I am holding my bow correctly and that the picture is black & white. I also like that it reminds me of the feeling I get when I play music for other people to enjoy!

PHOTO EXPLORATIONS

Look at the example of the girl playing the violin on the last page and try this photo assignment: Take a new or old photo of yourself participating in an activity you feel good about and glue it in the box or draw it below:
(See your answers on the last page for ideas.)

TITLE:

If this picture could talk, write what it might say here:

Explain what you like about this photo and think about why you like it:

NOTE: It feels good to be recognized for your accomplishments but your worth as a person is not measured by trophies, A's on your report card or even the number on the scale. Those things are examples of "external validation," which means feeling good about yourself for outside reasons such as what others think of you. "Internal validation" is feeling good inside of yourself and recognizing that you are a worthy, loveable person just because you are you, with or without these achievements.

CHAPTER 6
My Worries & Challenges

MY WORRIES:

Use this space to draw, write or make a collage of images that represent your current or past worries:

Write down a negative thought you tell yourself when you are worrying:
(For example, if you are worried about a test, a negative, unhelpful thought would be "I know I will fail the test!")

Now, write down a more helpful thought: (For example, "I may not get an "A" but I did review the study guide for an hour, and if I stay calm and focused, I will probably do okay. Even if I don't do great, my entire grade does not depend on this test.")

For the box below, draw, take or find a picture of how you appear when you feel stressed or worried:

"I feel stressed before I play catcher or go to bat because I'm afraid I may get hit by the ball or miss the ball, and the coaches will be disappointed in me."

Times when I feel this way:

Draw, take or find a photo of how you look when you are relaxed for here:

"After I bat and when the game is over, I am much more relaxed! I also feel very relaxed when I am playing with my cat & listening to music."

Times when I feel this way:

Write about the differences in these two images:

Peaceful Place – Find an image for this page of a space where you feel relaxed. Some possibilities could be your grandparents' home, your treehouse or a beautiful spot in nature. If you can't remember such a place, imagine what type of place would help you relax, and draw it.

When you are feeling stressed, sit quietly for a few moments and try to imagine being in this place while you focus on breathing slowly in through your nose and out through your mouth. Imagine the sounds, smells and sensations in this special place. If your mind returns to your worries, gently bring your thoughts back to your peaceful place and to your breath.

PHOTO EXPLORATIONS

MY CHALLENGE:

Write about something in your life that was difficult for you to do, but you have overcome or are in the process of overcoming. Some possibilities may be learning to ride a bike, adjusting to a new school or living with an illness or disability.

Write about how you overcame this or are currently working on it:

Who helped you get through this time period?

What did you learn from this experience that you believe will help you with future challenges in your life?

"The biggest obstacles you face are the ones in your own head...We place barriers on ourselves. If we can lift barriers, even set small goals, it can lift us up."
– Sandy Dukat, paralympic athlete, whose leg was removed at age 4 due to an illness

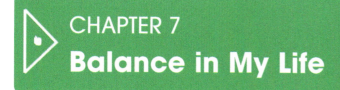

CHAPTER 7
Balance in My Life

"Live a balanced life – learn some and think some and draw and paint and sing and dance and play and work every day some."
– Robert Fulghum

When your life is in balance, it means that you are trying to take care of your body and your mind. It means that you are studying a reasonable amount but not obsessed with your school work so much that you are making no time for fun. It means sleeping enough, but not too much. It means spending time with your friends and family but also being comfortable spending some time alone. It means using technology some of the time but not being plugged in 24 hours per day. It means participating in some organized activities or sports that you enjoy, but not being booked with so many activities that you don't have time to breathe.

Scientists are learning how much the body and mind affect each other. Taking care of your body helps your mood and energy. Taking care of your mind may prevent high stress levels, which may cause physical problems such as poor sleep, headaches, stomach aches and muscle tension.

Coping skills are ways to help your mind by releasing stress and improving your mood. It is a good idea to use them on a regular basis, and they also help when problems arise in your life. They may help you work through intense emotions or just distract you from thinking about your problem for a little while, which also helps.

What coping strategies do you already use to take care of your mind and which ones would you be willing to try? Place a check by the ones that you already do and a star by the ones you are willing to try:

Drawing/Painting
Crafting
Scrapbooking
Taking photographs
Writing (journaling, poetry, songwriting, creating stories)
Yoga
Listening to music or searching for new music
Playing a musical instrument
Calling a friend
Spending time in nature
Reading
Cleaning or re-organizing your room
Playing a game
Taking a walk, run or bike ride
Swinging
Dancing
Watching a funny movie
Meditating
Listening to a relaxation recording
Playing with a pet
Taking a bubble bath or warm shower
Helping someone else

BODY CARE:

What are the things you already do to take care of your body?
Place a check by the ones that you already do and a star by the ones you are willing to try:

Staying away from drugs and alcohol

Drinking plenty of water and keeping caffeinated drinks to a minimum.

Sleeping Enough According to the National Sleep Foundation older kids and pre-teens need 10-11 hours of sleep, and teenagers need 8.5 to 9.5 hours (without their phones in the room). It's also important to not sleep too late on weekend days or nap during the day on a regular basis because it may disturb your sleep cycle.

Unplugging from all technology. We live in an amazing time with the ability to connect with others around the world. There are many ways technology has enhanced our living, learning and creativity, but living a balanced and more peaceful life means time away from all screens.

Skin Care: Washing your face in the morning and evening, moisturizing your body regularly with lotion and applying sunscreen.

Brushing and flossing your teeth regularly.

Eating Healthy: This means eating a variety of foods including fruits, vegetables, proteins, grains, dairy and fats; never skipping a meal; not overdoing foods with lots of sugar and fat though allowing yourself treats sometimes; saying "NO" to dieting and "NO" to weighing yourself, which may lead to unhealthy results such as thinking about food/weight all of the time and under/overeating. Instead, focus on an active lifestyle with balanced eating and trust that your body knows what to do when you nourish it.

Exercising or being active most days. This doesn't always mean going to a gym or P.E. class but it could include walking, skating, swimming, or dancing.
(Exercise is something that benefits your body and your mind. Not only does it improve strength and heart function but it releases chemicals in your brain, which improves mood, increases energy and reduces stress.)

PHOTO EXPLORATIONS

THANK YOU BODY!

We live in a culture where people focus more on how their bodies look rather than what they do. You don't have to join in, because we all know that it's what's on the inside that matters! Stay positive, and write a letter to your body expressing all of the things you appreciate about what it does for you. For example, you could thank your legs that let you walk, run and dance; your arms that allow you to hug and carry things; your brain that makes it possible for you to think, create and plan; and your voice that permits you to express your ideas. Next, make a promise to your body to take care of it by committing to recommendations on the previous page and/or coming up with other ways you may honor your body and help it stay healthy.

Dear Body....

40

CHAPTER 8
Meaning in My Life

In the previous chapter, you wrote a letter to your body. Now, continue the gratitude by describing what else in your life you appreciate.

THESE ARE A FEW OF MY FAVORITE THINGS:

Use the hearts on these pages to show or name your favorite book, possessions, song, television show, movie and quote. Then, explain why these are meaningful to you. As always, feel free to color and write outside the lines!

PHOTO EXPLORATIONS

42

WHO ARE YOUR ROLE MODELS?

These may be famous people or people you know personally and look up to such as teachers or grandparents. Use images and words to express the qualities you admire in your role models and what you have learned from the way they live their lives.

What qualities do your role models have that you hope to strengthen to help your future?
(For example, would you like to grow in your bravery, creativity, independence?)

What can you do now in your life to help yourself develop or strengthen the qualities that you admire in them?

PHOTO EXPLORATIONS

HELPING HAND!

Have you ever volunteered or raised money to help out people, an organization or a cause? If so, write about what you did and how it felt:

The media is filled with stories of kids and teens making a difference in their communities in a variety of ways. What causes interest you?

Are you passionate about fighting for the environment?

Does making and selling crafts to donate money to a cause or offering your time at a food or animal shelter interest you? There are many ways you can help improve our world! Volunteers frequently benefit themselves as well by gaining a sense of accomplishment, learning new skills and meeting new people.

45

PHOTO EXPLORATIONS

What about collecting books for a shelter?

Place or draw an image that represents a cause
that you believe in and would like to work on.

Explain why this cause is important to you:

If you would like to look for volunteer opportunities, talk to a parent about looking into: www.volunteennation.org. The website lists one-time and ongoing opportunities in the U.S. for teens and pre-teens starting at age 10!

CHAPTER 9
The Real Me - Who is the True You?

We all have many roles in our lives and behave differently with different people. If you are with your best friend, you may act silly but when you are with other friends you may act "cooler" or in a more mature manner. When you're alone with a parent in the daughter role, you may behave more childlike and when you are with a teacher, you may play the role of the serious student. So, who is the real you? All of your roles (daughter, granddaughter, sister, friend, student, athlete, performer, babysitter, etc.) contribute to who you are, and they all may feel like the "real you" at times.

Think about times when you feel most comfortable or most like the "real you" and create a self-portrait (or use a photo you already have) to show it. Maybe it will be a photo of you snuggling with your pet reading a book, running in a race or digging in a muddy garden. If you have trouble deciding on one image of the "real you", you may decide to take two photos, cut them in half and glue them together to illustrate this or make a collage of different pictures that show the true you.

Find, take or draw a picture of the "real" you for the box below and decorate it however you like:

TITLE:

In what ways does this show the real you?

How do you feel when you are being the real you?

What is it that you never want to change about the true you?

Who are the people in your life who you allow to see the real you & why?

What stops you from showing other people in your life this side of you?

CHAPTER 10
The Future Me

For your final assignment in this book, imagine your future.

"In 10 years, I would like to be a doctor living independently in a big city and maybe have a kitten."

For your future portrait, consider what you may want your life to look like in 5, 10 or 15 years. (You choose how many years ahead that you would like to imagine for your photo.) Think/write about these or other areas of your life:

CAREER/SCHOOL: What work would you like to be doing or do you plan to be in school? If you have no idea, that's fine! You will have many experiences ahead that may help you decide. Meanwhile, have fun playing with the possibilities.

FAMILY: Would you imagine being single or married at this age? Do you imagine having children and/or pets?

LOCATION: Would you like to live near the mountains or beach or maybe in a big city or small farming town?

Draw or take a self-portrait of a "grown up" you by selecting your outfit and finding (or drawing in) props if you like. You may want to use other images to collage a background for your portrait.

Create your future collage:

TITLE:

Today's Date: _____

Age I Am in This Photo: _____

PHOTO EXPLORATIONS

NEXT, REFLECT ON YOUR WORK.

How do you feel when you look at this collage?

What may be the positive and negative things about growing up?

What may get in the way of achieving what you want for your future life and how will you overcome these possible obstacles?
(For example, if you want to go to medical school, could grades and money possibly interfere in getting what you want?)

What actions can you take now and in the near future to help make this picture a reality?
(For example, if there is a subject in school that you are struggling with, could you ask a teacher for help? Could you start a savings account?)

PHOTO EXPLORATIONS

What words of encouragement do you need to remind yourself to help achieve your future dream? (This could be a quotation, lyrics from a song or your own words.)

If you were going to write a letter to your future self, what would you like to tell her?

53

If your future self was going to write a letter to you, what do you think she would say?

PHOTO EXPLORATIONS

Dear Readers,

I hope this was a fun and helpful experience for you. There is a blank page at the end of this book for whatever else you want to say. You also may want to purchase a blank book or sketchpad to design your own art/photo journal to continue to express yourself in the future. My wish for you is that no matter how busy you are, you continue taking time for techniques such as journaling, photography and artwork as creative ways to help you stay connected to your inner, true self and live a balanced life. Wishing you the best of luck on taking the steps to achieve your goals and remember:

**"It takes courage to grow up
and become who you really are."**

- E.E. Cummings

**"The one thing you have
that nobody else has is you.
Your voice, your mind, your story, your vision."**

– author Neil Gaiman

55

Acknowledgements:

Thank you to my mentor and friend, Judy Weiser, Director of the PhotoTherapy Centre, who has generously shared her passion and ideas with the world about how powerful and helpful personal photographs can be. Many of the assignments in this book have been inspired by, or adapted from her book, *PhotoTherapy Techniques: Exploring the Secrets of Personal Snapshots and Family Albums*. For more information about Judy — or Therapeutic Photography or PhotoTherapy Techniques — please visit http://www.phototherapy-centre.com and for more about her book, please see the "About the Book" page there (http://phototherapy-centre.com/phototherapy-techniques/about-the-book/).

My gratitude also goes out to my many other readers and contributors:
Melissa Biehl, Joanne Blum, Dori Bushman, Sharon and Chloe Chick, Dr. Malinda Dale, Pat Harris, Suzanne Landis-Goldstein, MSW, LCSW, Elizabeth Lyons, MSW, LCSW, Emma Lyons, Ann Mandelstamm, Robyn Meyer, Stacey, Grace and Claire Morris, Charlotte Oliva, Joy Seltzer and Cathy and Jack Davis of Davis Creative. Also, thank you to beautiful Camp Manitowa, the location where some of these photographs were taken during a recent Photo Explorations workshop.

Special thanks to my husband, Joel, and my extended family, friends and colleagues who support and encourage all of my endeavors!

I appreciate those who have shared their photos in this book as examples. Finally, thank you to the girls and women who have participated in Photo Explorations workshops and classes throughout the years and have taught me so much!

References:

Cummings, E.E. quoted in Burgess, M. (2015) *Enormous Smallness: A Story of E.E. Cummings.* Brooklyn, NY, Enchanted Lion Books.

Fulgham, R. (1986/1988). *All I Really Need to Know I Learned in Kindergarten.* New York, Villard Books, a division of Random House, Inc., and simultaneously in Toronto, Random House of Canada Limited.

Gaiman, Neil. "Keynote Address." Filmed May 17, 2012, from commencement, at The University of the Arts Philadelphia, PA. Accessed August 28, 2015, www.uarts.edu/neil-gaiman-keynote-address-2012

Goodreads.com, accessed May 1, 2015, http://www.goodreads.com/author/quotes/179335.Judy_Garland

"Paralympic Ski Champ Sandy Dukat's Trip to Sochi Canceled," Charity Goshay, CantonRep, March 9, 2014.

"Teens and Sleep," accessed April 3, 2015, http://sleepfoundation.org/sleep-topics/teens-and-sleep

Weiser, J. (1993/1999). *PhotoTherapy Techniques: Exploring the Secrets of Personal Snapshots and Family Albums.* Vancouver, Canada, PhotoTherapy Centre Press

Photo Credits:
All photos taken by Cathy Lander-Goldberg, Copyright CLG Photographics, Inc., except for the following:

Page 5 - Photo by Danielle Goldberg

Cover snapshot memory courtesy of subject.

Resources for Girls:
www.amightygirl.com
www.amysmartgirls.com
www.byoumagazine.com
www.discoverygirls.com
www.girlsinc.org
www.girlscouts.org
www.girlsontherun.org
www.Iamthatgirl.com
www.newmoon.com
www.operationbeautiful.com
www.volunteennation.org

(Please check with a parent before visiting these or any websites.)

Resources for parents:
http://selfesteem.dove.us/
(Also, see www.youtube.com Dove Selfie video.)
www.about-face.org
www.commonsensemedia.org
www.mindful.org
(Website contains techniques for children and adults.)
www.newmoon.com/adults-raising-girls
www.pbs.org/parents/parenting/raising-girls/

About the Author:

Cathy Lander-Goldberg is a photographer, educator, writer and licensed clinical social worker. Cathy grew up in St. Louis, Missouri and began taking photographs at age 14. At age 16, she achieved her goal of having her photos published in a local newspaper. Her career has been focused on helping girls and women find and express their voices, help themselves and use their talents to achieve their goals.

She is the director of Photo Explorations, which conducts workshops for organizations to help girls and women learn more about themselves through photography, writing and art. In addition, she uses expressive therapy techniques in her psychotherapy practice.

She also is the photographer for the traveling exhibition, RESILIENT SOULS. This display portrays courageous young women who have overcome a variety of issues early in their lives and follows them two decades later into adulthood.

Cathy lives in St. Louis, Missouri with her husband, daughter and golden retriever.

For more information on **Photo Explorations** workshops or the RESILIENT SOULS exhibition coming to your area, please visit www.clgphoto.com or e-mail photoexplorationsCLG@gmail.com. Information also available on Facebook and Instagram: **Photo Explorations**.

> You may choose to send a favorite photo you took for your book and write about how it makes you feel for possible publication on Instagram or the Photo Explorations Facebook page. If so, have a parent e-mail with permission to publish to photoexplorationsCLG@gmail.com.

What else do you have to say and show about your life?